Shameless Marketing

How to Be Outstanding While

Standing Out!

Brendon Sommers

R. Mickey Gorman

SHAMELESS MARKETING

*Being **outstanding** while standing out.*

Copyright © 2012 Small Business Development Services, LLC

ISBN: 1478139846

ISBN-13: 9781478139843

DEDICATION

To our parents, who guided us to where we are today.

CONTENTS

ACKNOWLEDGMENTS

There are a lot of people that need to be acknowledged for their contributions not only to this book, but our lives and our success.

Ed Davis
Tamara Patzer
Mike and Nina Strickland
Steve Chandler
Ben Graham
Jay Conrad Levinson
Mike Sisti
Larry Venable
John Gulick
Jim Cathcart
Harvey Mackay
Zig Ziglar
Jay Abraham

Shameless – (adjective) - lacking any sense of <u>shame</u>: immodest; audacious.

Marketing – Finding a need and filling it.

1. WHAT IS SHAMELESS MARKETING?

What started out as a humorous encouragement is starting to have a life of its own. I say it started as a humorous encouragement because Ed Davis and I took Summer Manda and her nonprofit organization, Positive Bounds, under our wings when we first met her at a chamber gathering. Ms. Manda had a hard time expressing herself without shedding tears. Growing up, she could not afford to participate in after-school programs. Friends and family stepped up to cover her expenses.

Ms. Manda decided there should be an organization to help kids today cover the costs of extracurricular activities, so she launched the nonprofit, Positive Bounds. She had a dream, but had no fundraising experience or any education for running a 501(c)(3) organization.

We jokingly told her she needed to be shameless in her efforts to promote what she was doing. The term caught on. People were using it at every function we attended. It may have helped that we would shamelessly market our last book, "It's Your Business."

We started talking about Shameless Marketing in our Entrepreneurial Academy classes. We told our "kids" (the Entrepreneurial Academy students) to be proud of what they do, and let the world know.

We were chatting about promoting our first book, It's Your Business... which is now available at Amazon.com, barnesandnoble.com and tower.com... (Did I mention that?)

We got into a discussion about what exactly is "Shameless Marketing." Here's what we came up with: **Shameless Marketing is being outstanding while standing out.** That pretty much sums it up.

Anybody can stand out by making a fool of themselves. That is not what I'm talking about.

I was in a great new restaurant in North Port last night and the YouTube video of Casey Anthony, who was acquitted of killing her baby, came on TV. Creating a viral video when you're considered an outlaw probably isn't wise. In this case, shame might be the better part of valor.

Good Shameless Marketing doesn't include stupidity.

As a business owner, Shameless Marketing is standing out, but doing so in a unique and outstanding manner. A few years ago during tax season, Liberty Tax Service started dressing folks up in Statue of Liberty outfits, and had them wave to people on the highway. At the time, it was unique, and the franchise has grown substantially. Seems now that every other business has caught the streetside waving bug —

while the technique is indeed shameless, it is no longer unique, and thus less effective.

Employees of The Ritz-Carlton Hotels are educated to anticipate customer needs. Employees go out of their way to pamper guests with extraordinary service. Several years ago, I was on a familiarization trip to the Ritz- Carlton Naples. I had my golf clubs with me. There was a Ritz-Carlton, Naples golf shirt waiting in my room when I checked in. The next day, I booked a three-night stay for 150 people, and utilized the hotel's meeting facilities. And I've worn the shirt on many golf outings, thus promoting the hotel.

The Ritz shamelessly promotes itself through extraordinary customer service and reaps the benefits of customers continuing to promote them long after the visit is over. What do you think was the return on the Ritz-Carlton's investment of a shirt?

Shameless Marketing is the attention part of the well-known marketing principle known as AIDA, an acronym for Attention, Interest, Desire and Action.

Shameless Marketing is what you do to get folks to focus on what you do.

If you are proud of what you do, let people know about it, and do it shamelessly.

Here's one more bit of Shameless Marketing: Make sure you visit our website and sign up for free newsletter on Shameless Marketing tips and ideas. www.shamelessmarketing.net

My dad always said that public relations was "doing good and getting credit for it." These days, hundreds of organizations flaunt the fact that they are attacking any successful business. It doesn't matter what you do to provide a product or service that people want. There are know-nothings out there willing to attack your efforts.

I can't understand why anybody would run for a public office these days. You put your name out there and it is open season on your entire life. I can remember reading an interview with Richard Nixon in which he was asked how he dealt with all the negative publicity he had received over his lifetime. He simply said he ignored it. You have to have armadillo skin these days to run for office.

Every day, businesses go far beyond the call of duty in providing products and services. Though our little small business has sponsored community activities and donated to local charities, for three years, not one of us has taken a paycheck. Why? Because our "why" from the start was to serve the communities in which we work and live. Everything that comes in goes back into the business or into the community. We worked our first year for a box of doughnuts.

There are hundreds of big and small businesses that quietly contribute to their communities. We could not do the Entrepreneurial Academies without the support of our sponsors. We make every effort to get them involved in our training programs in one way or another because we know we could not do what we do without them.

When we started this program, the city of North Port covered most of the expenses. We had no intention of starting a business, but the city wanted us to handle the whole process — and so we started a business.

Here we are teaching folks how to start a business, and we had no intention of starting one ourselves.

In case you are missing the point, we do good because it's the right thing to do. And, yes, we get some credit for it. That is the essence of public relations. If you don't toot your own horn, you would be amazed at how many folks will not hear it.

Developing your public relations strategy is a major portion of your marketing package. If you are successful and stick your head above the crowd, you will catch a few tomatoes in the face. Without question, tomato tossers are out there and they will find you.

No matter how well you do what you do, somebody will find something to complain about. Do it anyway, but be prepared for Negative Nellies and be ready to counter attack with a positive public relations strategy.

Awhile back, there was a rumor that McDonald's was using worm meat in its hamburgers. Company officials had a great response, which essentially went something like this: "Do you think we are stupid? Have you ever compared the price of a pound of worms to a pound of beef? Worms are way too expensive." End of slur — which in all probability was started by a disgruntled former employee.

Now, don't get me wrong, we really do screw up sometimes and need to own up to our mistakes. That, too, is part of public relations. Make it right and get the word out. If something negative occurs, admit it, fix it, and spread the news.

Most major corporations have established separate foundations that promote a cause. There are tax reasons for doing this, of course, but there are also public relations pluses that take a negative edge off the politics of envy of success.

Do good, but make sure you get some credit. That is public relations.

If you don't do it, who else will? OK, I realize that if you do anything that stands out in a small town culture folks will talk. The key is to be outstanding when you are standing out. If the definition of Public Relations is "doing good and getting credit for it," then how do you do that?

I've got to tell you I'm tired of timid. I don't want to lead a life of quiet desperation and go to my grave with my song still in me as Thoreau described it. Don't get me wrong, I've learned to shut up and listen and choose my battles wisely, but I also don't let an opportunity to speak up and express my point of view pass me by either.

Too many folks just go about their business and lead lives of quiet desperation. They don't want to "offend" anybody or disturb the status quo. Phooey! Disturb it, get off your lame butt and get the word out about the great stuff you are doing to make your world better. Oh, but you actually have to be doing something to make the world better to begin with. There's the rub.

So let's assume (yeah, I know, ass/u/me) that you are contributing to the betterment of humanity in some way. My former Father-In-Law was a janitor in a high school. He was a great guy and not only did he keep the school clean he interacted with the kids and did his part to keep them safe. You would never know that if I hadn't just told you. He was a go along, get along, person, just doing his job, collecting his pay, paying his bills, and going fishing. Most people had no idea what he did for a living. You would never hear a toot out of him.

The reason I point this out is he was happy just doing what he was doing. He was working for somebody else and taking home a paycheck. If you are a small business owner you don't have that luxury of being a part of the scenery in the background. You need to get the word out about the great things you make or do for others. You need to pull out your horn and toot, shamelessly!

I get a kick out of seeing folks I've worked with step up to the plate at Chamber meetings and speak out. I've had several of our "Kids" join me to do radio shows on WENG and they have done great. I really do take some pride in your Shameless Marketing. You believe in your business and you are not afraid to tell the world about the great things you are doing.

As my business partner, John Gulick, always says, you have to act like your mortgage depends upon your actions, because it does! He also points out that people in general like to do business with people they like. If nobody knows who you are it is darned hard to like you. It helps, of course, for you to be likeable. If you have that weaned on a pickle attitude, please stay out of my world, I don't need you and won't do business with you. If I do, it will only be once.

The best advertising you can get is word of mouth. You want folks talking about you in a good way. There's two parts to that equation, first, you have to stand out; second, you have to be outstanding. I guarantee you that if you are standing out by being a jerk, folks will talk about you. If you are contributing to the greater good and standing out you are controlling the message. If you are doing good and not getting credit for it you are missing the essence of good public relations.

I'm not talking about bragging. Dizzy Dean said, "It ain't braggin' if you can back it up." If you are a contributor to the betterment of your clients you are doing good and backing it up. Get the word out, toot your own horn. Don't die with your music still in you.

Dizzy also had this to say, "Sure I eat what I advertise. Sure I eat Wheaties for breakfast. A good bowl of Wheaties with bourbon can't be beat." *Let the music out!*

2. WHO LUVS YA?

If you accept the Pareto Principal that 80% of your business comes from 20% of your customers there are two things you need to do:

1. Identify the 20% and
2. Find new and creative ways to say "Thank YOU" to those 20%.

True story, ran into an old friend, Red Caveny, at a gathering one evening in Washington, DC of political types back in my DC days. We had a nice conversation and Red asked for my business card. A couple of days later I got a hand written thank you card from Red saying how great it was to see me again and chat. You should know that Red was making 10 times my income at the time and he was sending me a hand written thank you note. Guess that explains why he was making the really big bucks.

What is it about appreciation that we are missing out on? I'm talking about going beyond the expected. What can you do to show customer appreciation that makes a mark on the psyche of your clients that says they won't even think about using another provider of your services? Red had nothing to sell me but has developed a habit of writing personal notes to folks to stay in touch. I know from my lobbying years that you never know who can be an ally on a particular issue and Red was one of the best.

A simple hand written note can make a world of difference and very few people take the time to write one. It is a lost art and as such it is a great example of being outstanding while standing out. My Mom was a master at writing thank you notes. You did something she appreciated and she told you so in a hand written note. It is something we don't do enough of in a world of social media. We honestly don't even take the time for the most part to send a thank you email to most folks who do something we appreciate (like buy from us!).

There are hundreds of customer appreciation programs out there that can automate your thank you's to your customers. Honestly they are better than nothing but the chances of wowing your clients with an automated postcard on their birthday are not worth betting the ranch on. Remember we really want to make an impression on the 20% who provide 80% of our income.

How about a customer appreciation party? Consider an unexpected "baker's dozen" on top of their regular order. Don't just send a birthday card or email on their birthday, have a cake delivered. It is all about the wow and the appreciation for their business. Get your creative juices flowing. These folks are the life blood of your business. Say thank you in a way that means it.

3. MACKAY 66

Harvey Mackay has written several great books including Swim With the Sharks, Without Being Eaten. One of his smartest accomplishments was the development of his Mackay 66.

If you have not seen it, you can download it here http://www.harveymackay.com/tools/mackay-66/. It is a list of 66 questions all of his sales staff are required to complete on each of their customers. Some of the questions get fairly personal in nature and I'll bet it is next to impossible to complete the entire 66 questions. It is however, a great start for anyone who sincerely wants to provide outstanding customer service.

I realize most small business owners don't have the time to fill in all the blanks and may not even see the need for knowing all the answers to Mackay's questions. The purpose of the questionnaire is not to be nosey. It is designed to get a better understanding of the customer. Its purpose is to differentiate the sales staff of the Mackay Envelope Corporation from anyone else making envelopes.

I think it is safe to say that envelopes are fairly well a commodity when it comes to a purchasing decision. The more available a good or service is in the marketplace the more likely it comes down to a decision based on price. While price does matter, Mackay seeks to distinguish himself and his sales team by taking customer service to a higher level by personalizing each transaction.

Do you really need to know what a customer likes to eat, or if they served in the military, or their spouse and kids' names and birthdays? In one of his books, Mackay, talks about how one of his people landed a huge envelope account because of his knowledge of the customer. Let's face it, we like to do business with people we like. The salesman knew the purchasing agent's son was a big fan of baseball. He knew the son's birthday was coming up and knew his favorite team. On the son's birthday, the salesman showed up at the purchasing agent's office with an autographed baseball from son's favorite team. Who do you think got the next big order for envelopes?

It is not just about showing a kindness to a customer either. It is about getting to know what they need. There are several questions in the Mackay 66 that ask about how the customer thinks. What political persuasion is the customer and how strongly is their belief may not have a thing to do with what you are selling but you can pretty much count on losing a sale to the local Tea Party organizer if you show up at their office wearing an Obama button.

One of the things we talk about when teaching marketing is the understanding of People Dynamics and the Platinum Rule as opposed to the Golden Rule. The Platinum Rule states, "Do unto others as they wish to be done unto". It is all about understanding the needs of the customer and marketing is all about finding needs and filling them. The more you know, the better service you can provide.

You don't have to pry into people to dig out all the information on the questionnaire. Some of the questions are simply observations like does the buyer have an ego wall of pictures and plaques. Do they have diplomas on the wall? What school did they go to? Were they in a fraternity? There are many things you can learn about people just by being alert to their surroundings.

The survey is broken down into 7 major categories:

- ➢ Customers
- ➢ Education
- ➢ Family
- ➢ Business Background
- ➢ Special Interests
- ➢ Lifestyle
- ➢ The Customer and You

While the reality is you will probably never get into the detail that Mackay asks for in these categories, it probably would not hurt to have some knowledge in each of these categories for each of your customers.

The more you know about your customers the more ways you can find to be outstanding while standing out.

4. RECOGNITION

We all like to be recognized. Think about the last time you were called to the stage or the front of an audience to receive an award. Regardless of the type of award, it's still a pretty amazing feeling.

Remember the first time you set up an email account? If you're like me, you were probably checking it every 15 minutes to see who sent you a message. (Did someone recognize me?)

Being shameless is about getting positive recognition. When I was in high school I got recognized by the vice principal on a fairly regular basis. Those recognitions never made it to my resume´.

Abraham Maslow realized that recognition is an important aspect to our ego. It is the basis upon which a number of motivational and morale boosting programs are based.

This is what we want from our marketing efforts. Recognition. Instant recognition is better. Look at the following logos. Do you instantly recognize them?

Chances are you instantly recognized each of these images and were able to associate them with their products. (For the few that didn't – Nike, Pepsi and Cap'n Crunch). But it's not just images that can or should be easily recognizable. Tag lines, phrases and slogans all can be instantly recognizable.

> ➤ "When it Absolutely, Positively has to be there overnight"
> ➤ "30 minutes or It's Free"
> ➤ "Where's the beef?"

All of these tag lines seem to be ingrained in the American psyche, even though they haven't been used in recent ad campaigns.

But what do they all have in common? They are all very recognizable, but it didn't happen overnight. These companies spent a lot of money and it took a lot of time for them to develop the instant recognition we just demonstrated.

Think about politics where you live. More specifically, think about elections where you live. Did you ever wonder why campaigners hang out at polling places on the day of the election?

It is not so that the candidate can get you to understand his platform better. It is that the candidate knows that people (me and you), given unknown options from which to choose, will choose the one that comes to mind first. And the one that comes to mind first, is the one we saw last.

Have doubts? At the next election, look at the row of offices, city, county, and school board candidates on the ballot. How many of them do you know? How many of their stances and platforms are you familiar with? Who are you going to vote for? Chances are – the last flashy sign you saw before you walked in to the polling area.

Can you make this work for you and your business? Absolutely! Will it be easy? Probably not. Can you think like the marketing machine that is politics? OK, set your biases aside and just answer Yes.

Frequency and reach. You may have heard that phrase before. Mickey preaches it all the time. Get your message out often and to as many as possible. Oh and don't wait to get started. Instant recognition takes a long time to develop.

THERE ARE TWO THINGS PEOPLE WANT MORE THAN SEX AND MONEY: RECOGNITION AND PRAISE. -MARY KAY ASH

5. REMOVING PERCEPTIONS

Removing perceptions is about the ideas and perceptions that you have. Two of the biggest obstacles people and business owners run into is fear of failure and fear of people.

First, the bad news. Some of the things you try will not succeed and a lot of people will tell you no.

Now the good news. You are not alone. Just about any successful entrepreneur will tell you that he or she has failed at one time or another and many will tell you they have failed more than once. And every successful salesperson will tell you they had to work through all the nos to get to the yesses.

When you put everything on the line to start a business, failure is generally not an option. Attempting to do something or make something that is truly new and unique that people need brings with it a boatload of risk. Lots of things can go wrong. And I have to say, that's good. Fail early, often and quickly. Then move on.

When things are not working out as planned, you can do two things: adjust or accept that your plan failed and do something else.

Successful companies and people are not afraid to fail. If you suffer from a fear of failure you probably will not succeed. Actually, you will probably fail. This thinking also leads to the dreaded disease called the paralysis of analysis. You can research an idea to death when you might just be better off giving your idea a shot and see if it works. If it doesn't, get through the learning experience quickly. Of course, sometimes an idea takes time to gel, so if you try something and it isn't working as fast as you had hoped it would, you need to ask yourself these questions:

1) Am I heading in the right direction and just need to keep going? or,

2) Do I adjust what I'm doing rather than killing the concept? Often, you just have to keep plugging along until your product or service gains critical mass.

Most folks who are afraid of people are afraid of being told "no." They use the excuse that they really don't want to bother anybody. If you have a product or service that folks really need and want, how are you bothering them by helping them get what they need? As a salesman, I know that everyone is not going to tell me yes when I offer them an opportunity. It is usually more stressful on the person saying no than it is on me because I don't take rejection personally. If I'm offering them the greatest thing since "sliced bread" and they don't want it, it is their loss, not mine.

Speaking of sliced bread, in 1912, Otto Frederick Rohwedder, from Davenport, Iowa, invented the Rohwedder

Bread Slicer. Bakers were reluctant to pre-slice their bread as they worried the slices would go stale quicker. Mr. Rohwedder persisted, including attempting to keep the slices held together with hat pins, which didn't quite work out. It was not until 1928, when he enhanced his slicer with a wax paper wrapping system and found a baker by the name of Frank Bench in Missouri who was willing to give it a try that his idea took off. On July 7, 1928, the first loaves of Sliced Kleen Maid Bread hit the shelves and sales took off. In 1930, Wonder Bread hit the stores and the rest is history.

The point is that even though it took Mr. Rohwedder 16 years and some failed adjustments, like hat pins, to make his program work, he knew his idea was a winner and if he had to go to another state and meet new people, he did it. No FoF, no FoP for Mr. Rohwedder.

Now I can remember when I was a kid, we had a single slice bread slicer because the Wonder Bread came in such thick slices that you could put it in this contraption and run a knife down the middle and make two slices to make a not so bread-laden sandwich. Eventually Wonder Bread caught on and made an adjustment to sell "thin-sliced" bread. Does that make it even greater than sliced bread?

Take your perceptions out of the picture. Those are what usually stop people from moving forward. The thought of rejection or a painful experience is almost always far worse than the reality of it.

For example, let's look at people that are telemarketers. It can be extremely difficult to pick up the phone and call 200-

400 people a day. The reality is the worst that can happen (assuming you are following solicitation laws) is the person will say some unpleasant things to you. You can hang up on them. Done. Now go on to the next. Much easier if you just do   and   don't   think   a   lot   about   the   outcomes.

6. SHAMELESS NETWORKING

The first rule of attending a networking event is that you need to be prepared to network. That may sound stupid but I see folks at these events all the time who show up without business cards or brochures or something to remind the new folks they meet who the heck they are, really!

Networking events are the equivalent of a cold call. The folks who attend them are open to meeting and greeting new people. As with a cold call, this is not the time to be selling. It is time to learn about their needs and who they are and to share with them your needs and who you are.

This is not a time to be shy. If you see a new face in the crowd step up and introduce yourself. Exchange business cards with them and give them your 30 second elevator speech. It is the reason you are there (other than the free booze and food at most of them).

I'm joking about the free booze and food but it amazes me the number of folks who fill up a plate and go sit with their friends during networking events. The purpose of a networking event is to circulate and meet new people. Sure it is great to re-connect with old pals but this is a business opportunity. Take advantage of it (unless of course you are starving because your business is doing poorly because you are not marketing and this is your only meal of the week).

Then comes the really important part, if you think you have a match with what you offer and their needs, for heaven's sakes follow up with them! While I was writing this I realized I had met someone the other day and stuck her card in my wallet. I fished it out and stopped writing to call her. It turns out she is not the decision maker for her business. She did give me the name of the person who is and took my number again as well as the website information and said she would pass it up the food chain. I don't want to be accused of not practicing what I preach.

Set a goal before you go to a networking event. It doesn't have to be a big one. For example, my goal at a networking event is to meet at least 5 new people. Yes I've heard folks say the same people go to the same events all the time. Many folks do, but there are always new faces in the crowd. Hunt them down and get to know them.

Are there other things you can do to be outstanding while standing out? Sure there are, for example the North Port Chamber had a membership drive kick-off with a super hero theme. Rob Nelson and Jill Luke showed up in super hero costumes. We give out copies of our books as door prizes at chamber events. Steve Burnett does themed humorous introductions. There are hundreds of unique things you can do to get the crowd's attention in a unique and positive way.

And that is key, it needs to be unique and positive. While it can be humorous, it should not be offensive. Always remember you are representing your business. Stand out but do it outstandingly.

"The successful networkers I know, the ones receiving tons of referrals and feeling truly happy about themselves, continually put the other person's needs ahead of their own." -Bob Burg

7. WHY NOT YOU?

Every year, around 500,000 new small businesses get started in this country. Somebody with a dream and a technical ability starts a business, and over half of them fail. There is a reason for that, they don't know a darned thing about cash flow. There are a whole lot of other things they don't know about, but I'm all for every one of them. Pursue your dream. Give it a shot, you have about a 50/50 chance of succeeding. A flip of the coin, that's a reality.

I've owned several businesses that I've quit. Yup, I've failed. Been there, done that. Worked my butt off and it didn't happen. But I've tried again and again, maybe I'm stupid but I don't think so. That didn't work, NEXT! That is the mentality of an entrepreneur. Some of the most successful folks have failed many times but the one thing they never gave up on was themselves.

I love that attitude in people, "I believe in me." Why not you? I can't tell you the number of folks I've met who have a dream but they don't have the guts to step out and make their dreams a reality. Hell yeah, you got a shot at failure, but do you have what it takes to make the leap and make it happen?

Samuel Pierpont Langley was the Secretary of the Smithsonian in Washington, DC. Based on the success of his Aerodrome 6 unmanned flyer he was given an award by the War Department of the United States of $50,000 which was matched by the Smithsonian to develop a plane capable of manned flight. His prototype was based on his 6 model which was not steerable so he thought it best that his test flights should be over water. He spent half his funding building a houseboat with a catapult to launch his craft.

On October 7, 1903, Charles Manly bravely boarded the craft and prepared to fly. He was catapulted off the boat directly into the freezing Potomac River. Manly tried again on December 8, 1903 and succeeded in getting another dunking

in the icy Potomac.

The War Department's report concluded, "we are still far from the ultimate goal, and it would seem as if years of constant work and study by experts, together with the expenditure of thousands of dollars, would still be necessary before we can hope to produce an apparatus of practical utility on these lines," once again proving that government intelligence is an oxymoron.

December 14, 1903, only 6 days later, two brothers who owned a bicycle shop, Orville and Wilber Wright, made their first attempt at flight in a contraption they had put together at their own expense of about $1,000. With Wilber at the controls the plane failed to fly and was damaged in the effort. The brothers went back to work and 3 days later, this time with Orville at the helm, the "Flyer" did just that, it flew for 12 seconds covering a whopping 120 feet. In later trials the brothers managed to stay aloft for as much as a full minute.

Two guys, with no college education, no big government backing, and a dream succeeded where the experts had failed. Why not you? Your dream may not change the world like the Wright brothers did, but it might change your community. Acting on your dream will definitely change your life.

I know there are dreamers out there who have great ideas, ideas that given time can succeed. Step out and shamelessly follow your dream. Why not you?

8. MOVE IT OR LOSE ME

Repetition is good. Redundancy – not so much. We wrote about Zig Ziglar and his consistent message. Repetition – good. But he changes the stories and analogies he uses to convey that message. He keeps it from being redundant (and boring).

Businesses need to do the same thing. Study some of the commercial advertising you see. Much of it is repeated over and over – and then changed. If even only slightly. They may just add an additional element to break up the monotony of the original campaign. Take GEICO. They introduced the GEICO gecko years ago. Repetition, good. Very popular and very memorable. But after all those years, maybe starting to get a little stale. So they introduced Maxwell the pig. (He's the one the screams WHEEEEEEE all the time). Still memorable. Sometimes fun. But fresh.

We have a lot of water in Florida, the Gulf, the ocean, ponds, lakes, rivers and canals. During the non-rainy season (drought time) you can see algae and pond scum accumulating in some of these bodies of water. Yet when a fresh source of water (rain, springs, etc) is introduced into it, the algae and scum clears and life in that body of water flourishes again.

Which reminds me of the Law of Diminishing Returns. The Law of Diminishing returns is a law affirming that to continue after a certain level of performance has been reached will result in a decline in effectiveness. I often refer to this as the "Hot Dog Rule" (mostly because that is the analogy I learned in college).

Let's say you like hot dogs. You sit down and eat a hot dog. And then another. And another. And another. And another. At some point your fondness for hot dogs will lessen and you'll get sick of eating them. It works the same way with your marketing.

Consumers, or your clients, get tired of the same thing constantly. People tend to have short attention spans. People like variety.

Now add some ketchup to those hot dogs. You can eat more. When you get tired of the hot dogs with ketchup, add relish. Then mustard. Then onions. Just keep it from being over saturating and boring. Mix it up occasionally. Throw some spice on the rice.

Get my interest – don't get me tuned out. Don't lose me.

9. WHO OR WHAT ARE YOU MARKETING?

We know by now that being shameless is about being outstanding while standing out. This takes consistency and persistency. Changing course or changing strategies frequently may not be the best idea.

When I think about someone being shameless in a consistent manner, Sir Elton John comes to mind. He is instantly recognizable with outrageous glasses and eye catching costumes. He is also musically brilliant. But there are countless other musically brilliant people in the world, just as there are countless other great salespeople or dentists or roofers or any other profession.

Sir Elton helped himself get recognition by using the sometimes outlandish get ups, but he did it consistently and persistently. He did it for every show and he did it for decades. (We are not suggesting you need to don a costume.)

You may have heard of a gentleman by the name of Zig Ziglar. Mr. Ziglar is arguably the greatest motivational speaker in the world. He didn't get that way by changing his message every few months. His messages have been consistent for as long as I can remember. The stories he uses to convey those messages may change with his experiences, but he has been delivering the same messages for a very long time (persistency).

But before you can start being consistent and persistent, you must clarify. You must be clear, to yourself and to your audience, who or what you are marketing.

Are you marketing yourself? We know that people tend to do business with people they know, like and trust.

Are you marketing your business? Brand awareness can play in key role in purchasing decisions.

Are you marketing your product(s)? Something has to get sold for anything to happen.

I've been to countless events, meetings and just meeting people on the airplane, that left me confused about their message. One sure way to not get business is to confuse people. We are inundated every day with news, information, advertising, social media and our own lives. The clearer we can make our message, the better for everyone.

It not only has to be a clear message, but the right message. I can remember, once upon a time, when I was stressing me. My talents, my skills, my personality (yes I do have one), what uniqueness I brought to the table. The reality is, I should have been focusing primarily on the firm I worked for. They had instant name recognition. One of the best reputations in the industry. Nationwide.

I could have used all of that and utilized their strengths to transfer recognition to me. Wow! This great company was smart enough to hire this guy. I know they are a prestigious firm. He must be good.

But alas, we live and learn. I didn't do that. So I was clearly not espousing the right message at the time.

And sometimes who or what you are marketing needs to be tweaked for specific audiences and specific tasks. For example, most of the time I promote our small business coaching services, but at appropriate times we promote our Entrepreneurial Academies. Consistent messages with different audiences.

Stay consistent. Be persistent. Be Shameless about it.

"I DON'T EXACTLY KNOW WHAT I MEAN BY THAT, BUT I MEAN IT."
— J.D. SALINGER

10. YOU GOTTA BELIEVE

The Law of Attraction states that you attract into your life that which you think about. Earl Nightingale, in his breakthrough recording, "The Strangest Secret" (http://video.google.com/videoplay?docid=-8448018326921957619#) summed it up as "You become what you think about".

If it is that simple, why do we all not have what we want? If all I have to do to attract what I want in my life is to think about it, why aren't I rich? Well, there is another part of the equation. Nightingale also states that "Whatever the mind of man can conceive and believe it can achieve." It is not enough to just think about it you have to believe, and there's the rub.

You may need money to pay your bills and you are constantly thinking about money. But are you really thinking about attracting more money or are you cogitating on how in the hell am I going to pay my cell phone bill this month? Just thinking about something doesn't make it so. You have to believe and act on your belief.

The other point Nightingale makes is that we are conformists. We do what everyone else does because that is the way we were brought up. He quotes a study that asked people why they get up and go to work. Most had no special reason, it's just how things are done, or to make money. Only 1 in 20 said because they love what they do and can't wait to do it some more!

We all know people who are just working to make money. They may even hate what they do day in and day out and still get up each day grudgingly and do it. They might even have a dream tucked away on what Dennis Waitley calls "Someday Isle" as in someday I'll win the lottery or someday I'll buy a new car. These folks are living a life of "quiet desperation" according to Thoreau, and all they need to do to change it is to change their thoughts.

Nightingale also points out that money follows service. You get back from prosperity in accord with what you add to prosperity. Ecclesiastes 11:1 says "Cast thy bread upon the waters; for thou shalt find it after many days." What The Preacher is talking about has nothing to do with soggy bread. What vibrations you give off return to you either positively or negatively. Those vibrations are your thoughts and your thoughts are what attract things to you. You are constantly becoming what you think about.

If you are not happy, nobody can change that but you, nobody caused it but you. Wayne Dyer tells the story of the farmer mending his fence by the road when a car pulls up and the driver rolls down his window and asks, "I'm thinking about moving to the town up ahead. What are the folks like in town?" The farmer asks, "Well what were the folks like in the town you are coming from?" The driver replies, "They were surly, always in a hurry, not very friendly, to be honest." The farmer says, "That's pretty much the way folks are in the town here."

Shortly thereafter another car pulls up and asks the same question of the farmer who gives him the same question. This time, the driver answers, "Wow, I'm going to miss those folks, they were special people with hearts of gold. They would literally give you the shirts off their backs." The farmer says, "That's pretty much the way folks are in town here too." You get what you are looking for and what you think is your reality.

Positive belief then is the key ingredient in attaining your dreams. Decide what you really want in your life and write it down. Don't type it; actually take out a piece of paper and a pen and write it down. Nightingale suggests you write it on a 3 by 5 card and keep it in your pocket and look at it several times a day for at least 30 days. He also suggests you turn the card over and add the words from the Sermon on the Mount (Matthew 7: 7-8)

"Ask, and it shall be given you;
Seek, and ye shall find;
Knock, and it shall be opened unto you;
For everyone who asketh receiveth;

And he that seeketh findeth;
And to him that knocketh it shall be opened."

Open your mind to the possibilities. Dream big and believe in your dreams as if you already have them. Change your thinking and change your life. Then all you have to do is ask. You gotta believe. When you believe, everyone else will start to.

11. HOW PROUD ARE YOU?

Once upon a time there was such a thing as pride. Pride in one's school, pride in one's appearance, pride in the job you did. What are you proud of? How proud are you? Proud enough to shout from the rooftops? To let the world know?

When you develop pride in something, it shines through and gets noticed. Whether it's pride in your job, your product, your appearance, your kids or grandkids, the way you maintain your lawn, it reflects positively on you. Our friend, Ed Davis, one of the founders of our Entrepreneurial

Academies, would show slide after slide of his grandkids during class. Proud? You bet he is! And he has no problem letting the world know it.

One of my favorite books, *The Wealth Within You* by Elmer Wheeler, cites numerous examples of taking pride in one's work and the positive results derived from it. One story that stands out for me is that of Charles Markham. Mr. Markham started out as janitor for the Illinois Central Railroad. He didn't disillusion himself about his job. He knew he was "just" a janitor. But he took pride in his work and did it very well. Not surprisingly, he got noticed. He took pride in the work, regardless of what the work was. He got promoted. He took that same pride to his next position. And to the one after that. All the way to becoming the head of the railroad.

You would be hard pressed to find a prouder group than the United States Marine Corps. Ooh-Rah! How often do you see a former Marine? Very rarely. Even those no longer serving tend to identify themselves as Marines, not former Marines. That's pride.

I was at a restaurant having dinner a few months ago. It was a chain restaurant that I frequent. This was the first time, and likely last, that I ate at this particular location. The lighting was dark, the carpet was dirty, the service was slow and unprofessional. By the time I got served, it would not have mattered if it was the best meal I had ever eaten. My mood was set by the experience. If they take so little pride in how the restaurant looks and their customer care, how much pride are they going to have in the food they are serving? Where pride shines through for you and gets you noticed, lack of pride can do the same, only with less than positive outcomes.

But what about you? Are you embarrassed of or proud to work where you're at or do what you do or sell what you sell?

I took a job once, that on paper looked to be that dream job. Office paid for, assistant paid for, marketing paid for, no prospecting. As it turned out, I was actually embarrassed to tell people who I worked for. Not an ideal situation to sell in. That lasted for about a month.

Conversely, I was asked to join Small Business Development Services, LLC as a partner to replace one of the retiring partners. I am one the biggest cheerleaders and promoters of this company and our programs. I am proud to work with them to accomplish what we do for small businesses.

How proud are you? Stand out. SHOUT IT OUT!!!

Vanity and pride are different things, though the words are often used synonymously. A person may be proud without being vain. Pride relates more to our opinion of ourselves, vanity to what we would have others think of us.

JANE AUSTEN,

12. IT'S NOT PERSONAL. IT'S JUST BUSINESS

OK. If you've started your own business, I know everything seems personal, but it's not. If you work for a business, things still frequently feel personal, but they're not.

A number of years ago, when I was managing a store for a large electronics retailer, I had a customer come in making some pretty unreasonable demands. After about 20 minutes of back and forth "conversation", the customer tried to make it personal. She decided to try insulting me and my earning capacity. Something about being a minimum wage corporate drone. I was very tempted to pull up my W-2 and push it under her nose, but instead I calmly stated that the product was abused and was not covered by any warranty on earth and that what I earn has no bearing on that and will not change that.

When it comes to promoting our business or ourselves or our products or services, we need to have the same mentality – It's not personal, it's just business.

When you try or do something new or something creative or something out of the ordinary or even something basic that everyone should do but doesn't, people will look at you funny or say that it is stupid or that it won't work.

This happens primarily, I think, because people don't want to be reminded that they could or should be doing what you ARE doing. Sometimes those voices you hear will come from inside your own head. "This is stupid." "This will never work." "Nobody has ever done this before." "This is embarrassing".

You can move past these thoughts. Remember, it's not personal. It's not about you. It's about the end result. Will it get you greater positive recognition? Will it get you more sales? What is your desired end result from your activity? If you keep that goal in mind, not only will the voices in your head be quieted, but the external voices will have less and less impact and influence on you.

No one actually expects you be the next Mr. Spock. We all get emotional at times. We all have buttons that people push (and sometimes I think they like to push them). I understand that setbacks, complaints and the like feel like a personal attack, just as winning awards and contests feel like personal victories. They are all inconveniences on the way to the end result.

What is the "end result?" For me there are several. One is getting an appointment. Another is inking an agreement. You decide what the results need to be. You decide what speed bumps will distract you from reaching those results. Don't take it personally. It's just business.

In the Odyssey, by Homer, Odysseus, on reaching the island of the Sirens, has himself tied to the mast of his ship and uses beeswax to plug the ears of his sailors to protect them from the Sirens' song. The song they sang was so appealing that sailors would be drawn to it and crash their ships into the rocks and die.

I was listening to a talk on TED.com and the speaker, Daniel Goldstein, was discussing how being strapped to the mast is a metaphor for what is called today a commitment devise. It is something we do to keep us on track from being distracted from our goals, the Siren song.

Anyone who has made a commitment knows there are distractions, for example Christmas cookies and weight loss promises. The small business owner hears the Siren song over and over again when a deadline is due and there are many distractions. I know more than one small business owner who has had to strap themselves to the mast to get past Distraction Island.

The hardest hit are those who operate a home based business. When you work where you live you are surrounded by your life. The phone rings, the kids need something, you have to make dinner, the list goes on and on. When you are on a deadline to get a project completed and are running out of time, sometimes you might literally have to strap yourself to your work and ignore any distractions.

Goldstein says that it is a battle between your "present self" and your "future self". He points out that the future self is not even present in the commitment battle. The future you is only a dream either positive or negative. It could be the vision of future wealth and a great retirement or it could be that if you don't get the work done right now you will lose a major client and not be able to make your mortgage payment. Either way, the commitment you bring to the task, will determine the outcome for the future you.

Don't kid yourself, the Sirens will be singing the whole time loud and strong. You have to take little Billy to his football game and there's that show on television you don't want to miss.

Goldstein was writing a book and he determined he needed to write 5 pages a day. His commitment devise was that if he didn't do it he would have to give away $5. It can be as simple as putting a rubber band around your arm and when you feel yourself getting distracted, give it a snap. (Ouch!)

The point is, whatever your motivation, you need to focus on the task at hand. If strapping yourself to the mast helps, do it. You are the locus of control. If you need a commitment devise, find a picture of what you want in your future and put it up on your wall. You might even drown out the Siren song with some headphones and relaxing music as you work. In any event, the vision you create in the future is in the hands of your present self. Stay off the rocks and "*Get 'er done!*"

13. SHAMELESS CLIENT CARE

You hear it all the time. "The customer is king." "Our service is second to none." "Satisfaction is job one." Then you go out and find that the great customer service message seems to be more of a slogan than a culture.

Have you ever gone into a business with a concern and heard some of these responses? "We can't do that." "Our policy doesn't allow it." Or one of my favorites – "The manager has to handle that." (And you know the manager is on vacation).

Shameless marketers know that a client's perception is the client's reality. They don't really care what the company policy is – they just want their issue resolved.

We just read Jay Abraham's book <u>Getting Everything You Can Out Of All You Got.</u> Jay offers copies of his two books online for free. There's a reason he is doing that. He wants to go back to the way he started his business by working one on one with clients in exchange for a percentage of their business. He is using his books as a loss leader for developing new clients.

There's a great chapter on knowing the lifetime value of a typical customer. If you have a product or service that is one and done, that's the life of the deal. However if you have or

do something that people need on a regular basis your objective should be to retain their trust for life. Your focus should be on not just getting them in the door for the first time but to keep them. Ritz Carlton Hotels, for example, know the lifetime value of their typical customer is $250,000. Knowing that, they go out of their way to do whatever it takes to keep their clients happy and keep them coming back for more.

Probably the premier company at practicing outstanding customer service is the Ritz Carlton Hotel chain. While the architecture of each property in any part of the world attempts to adapt to the flavor of the area, the persistent devotion to "wow" their guests never changes. It begins in their hiring practices. Ritz doesn't hire employees, they select team members. The motto of all team members is "We are ladies and gentlemen serving ladies and gentlemen." Even new hires can spend up to $2,000 of the hotel's money if need be to quickly solve any problem a guest may have. Any team member is empowered to be a problem solver and if they hear of a problem they own it and are responsible for solving it. The company posts on their website their "Gold Standards" and at the beginning of each shift team members in each department review them and discuss them. They have estimated that the average customer, over the course of their lifetime, will spend over $250,000 utilizing their services which include, in addition to great hotel rooms, world class spas, restaurants, gift shops, and several golf courses.

In addition, if you have ever been a Ritz guest, they keep a permanent file on you in their worldwide computer system so the next time you visit they can be ready with all of your needs. Want a cold bottle of beer and a dish of peanuts when you arrive? It will be ready and waiting when you check into your room on your next visit without even having to ask.

But Shameless Marketers also know that Shameless Client Care is about much more than resolving client problems.

My good friends Mike and Nina Strickland, own The Strickland Financial Group in Fort Myers, Florida. They and their staff epitomize Shameless Client Care. When they bring on a new client they have only one rule – the client must be nice.

They also seem, in my observations, to have two unwritten rules:

1. Treat each client as if they are your best and only client. Think about it. How do you or your staff treat your best clients? How would you treat them if they were your only client? Chances are you treat them as royalty. Is there any good reason YOU shouldn't be treating your clients like royalty?
2. Mike, Nina and the team anticipate their clients' needs. They take a proactive approach rather than reactive. If you anticipate client needs and desires, you can work to make them non-issues.

I think what makes their client care so great, is that they find and solve real and potential problems for their clients. The clients become like family. When was the last time someone arranged a group cruise and invited you? Or invited you to a Christmas party at their house? Or simply got your credit card company on the phone to check for identity theft, because your credit card didn't go through?

They embody the saying-"Treat people the way they want to be treated." Everyone is special to them. This is truly Shameless Client Care.

14. FOLLOW UP, FOLLOW UP, FOLLOW UP

It is not just enough to get people's attention with your Shameless Marketing, you need to follow up. I'm amazed at the efforts businesses make to get the attention of potential buyers and then sit back and wait for them to make the next move.

I did a study a few years ago. It was simple and probably quite unscientific, but the results were glaring. And I still find that the results continue to hold constant.

The experiment consisted of simply exchanging business cards with other professionals at various events. Over a period of eight months, I exchanged more than 480 business cards. The astounding results were that of those 480 plus other professionals, only six followed up with me. And that was even after I followed up with them. That's an appalling 1.25 percent. Lower than the expected return for a generic direct mail piece. How much business is being left on the table? I can only imagine that this phenomenon is not isolated. If these other professionals are not following up with me, chances are good that they are not following up with a lot of others.

Why do you go to networking events when you don't follow up with viable contacts?

One of our students took my message to heart and made follow-up calls to four people she met at a recent chamber meeting. She has appointments to meet with a couple of them and will develop relations with them that will pay off over time.

We all know that we should follow up, don't we? Some of the barriers, I think, to people following up are the why, how long and how often questions. Why do we need to follow up? The simple answer would be that it is just good business. But that's kind of like your parents saying, "Because I said so." Yeah, you do it for a while because they said so, but then it trails off. The less simple answer is that a buying decision, if the need is present usually takes 5-12 touches. A touch is anytime someone comes in contact with you or your marketing message. So the initial contact is one touch. The follow up call, email or thank you note is another. Your newsletter is another. Your ad in the paper is another. And you follow up and follow up and follow up. Will everyone buy from you or use your services? Absolutely not. Will more people buy and use your services and refer others to you because you stayed in touch and stayed front of mind for them? Absolutely.

Follow up is the key to making your business survive. 60% of your marketing efforts should be with existing or former clients. I'm not making that up, Jay Levinson of Guerilla

Marketing will tell you as much. I was chatting with a student recently and I told her to call all of her former clients (most are a one time sale) and ask if they are happy with their purchase of her products and services and if they needed anything else. But most importantly I told her to ask if they knew anybody else who could use their services!

Follow up is not just to see if you have done your job to the complete satisfaction of your clients, it is to get referrals. Referrals are the pre-touch you didn't have and the first of your 5 to 12 touches you need to make 80% of your sales. The other 40% of your marketing effort is 30% to your identified target market and 10% to the general public.

Think about the last time you bought a car. Did you buy the first car you looked at the first time you saw it? Probably not. Chances are you may have seen an ad on TV, then in the paper, then went to look at a car, then to another dealership, and maybe another. Multiple touches before you bought.

So when do you throw in the towel and say enough is enough? Do you follow up for 6 months or a year or 5 years or 10 years?. It depends. Unfortunately, there really is no cookie cutter answer for that. Every client or prospect and every marketing campaign and every sale is different.

If part of your follow up process (you do have a process, don't you) involves automated email or newsletters, people that don't want to hear from you will unsubscribe and disqualify themselves. For the rest, my advice is, assuming the people are within your target market, keep following up until they tell you to get lost. But be cautioned, you need a reason to follow up like a new product or service, a special you are running, a holiday, birthday or other event, an article that will be of interest to them, etc. On the other hand, if they haven't opened any of your emails for a year, it may be time to cut them loose.

Now that you know why following up is critical to your success, take action and do it. Need a place to start? Send a handwritten thank you note to everyone you've spoken with in the last 30 days.

15. THREE RULES OF SHAMELESS MARKETING

It may seem that Shameless Marketing wouldn't have any rules. After all, it is shameless. But without some rules we'd have anarchy (and the FCC and courts would be overwhelmed).

So we have three simple, easy to remember rules:
1. It must be legal.
2. It must be ethical.
3. It must be effective.

Remember that just because it's legal, that doesn't mean it's ethical. And just because it's legal AND ethical, that doesn't mean it will be effective. Let's take a look at these 3 rules individually.

1. IT MUST BE LEGAL. One would think that this would be a no-brainer, but there is a lot that can go into being legal. (The former financial advisor in me is obligated to tell you that we are not attorneys and do not provide legal advice.)

Frequently, I find that businesses and people hear or see something for so long and with such frequency, that thoughts of its original source are forgotten, and they start to adopt it as their own. Be careful not to infringe on trademarks, patents, copyrights, images or other intellectual property, unless you have express permission and cite the source.

If you've ever seen the Eddie Murphy movie "Coming To America" you'll appreciate this line from John Amos:

"Look…me and the McDonalds people got this little misunderstanding. See they're McDonalds…I'm McDowells. They got the Golden Arches, mine is the Golden Arcs. The got the Big Mac, I got the Big Mick. We both got two all beef patties, special sauce, lettuce, cheese, pickles and onions, but their buns have sesame seeds. My buns have no seeds."
DON'T INFRINGE.

Oh yes… if you are supposed to have a license or permit, please get it.

2. IT MUST BE ETHICAL. Again, this sounds like a no brainer. But ethics seem to be extremely subjective. There are entire fields of study devoted to ethics. Obviously, there is need. I like simple. Do the right thing, even when no one is watching. If I can run it by my wife and my parents and still be able to sleep at night, it's probably OK. Does that mean everyone will be OK with it? Probably not.

You can't please all the people all the time. You don't have to. Rely on or develop your own ethical compass.

3. IT MUST BE EFFECTIVE. This rule can seem like a Catch-22. (A phrase derived from the novel of the same name by Joseph Heller). It is difficult to test the effectiveness of a strategy without doing it for a some length of time. But if it's not effective, do you really want to continue doing it? One fix for this conundrum, is to have multiple, staggered

strategies, so that if something is not effective you can stop doing it without having to restart the entire process.

For example, the following diagram explains a simplified staggered calendar:

Method	Goal	Jan	Feb	Mar	Apr	May	Jun	Jul	Aug	Sep	Oct	Nov	Dec	TTL
Email Flier		x			x			x			x			
Ad in local Paper			x			x			x			x		
Networking Events		x	x	x	x	x	x	x	x	x	x	x	x	
Sale				x			x			x			x	

Three simple rules. Legal. Ethical. Effective. Now go get 'em!

"WE STARTED OFF TRYING TO SET UP A SMALL ANARCHIST COMMUNITY, BUT PEOPLE WOULDN'T OBEY THE RULES."
— ALAN BENNETT, *GETTING ON*

16. COLD CALLING SUCKS

I once had a hotel sales executive tell me that her sales manager told her she needed to get out and make more cold calls. My response was, "yeah, that's so he doesn't have to go out and make them himself". Most people in sales, unless they are the most people friendly folks in the world, hate making cold calls. The reason they hate them is they are trying to close the sale on the first meeting.

Only 2% of sales are made on the first meeting which means that you will have to make 50 calls to make one sale. OK if you are selling big dollar, high commission stuff it might be worth it. Mostly it is a waste of time for little return on investment.

I've said it before and I'll say it again, if you are trying to make a sale to someone you have just met and know nothing of their needs and how your goods and services can meet their needs you are just spinning your wheels and hoping to get lucky. It is a major waste of not only your time, but the people you call on also.

Spending all that time getting rejections is also a downer. How many times a day can you get turned down without it becoming a drag to your spirit. Even though I've been known to do my fair share of smiling and dialing to set up appointments, if I had to work as a telemarketer for a living I'd probably blow my brains out. Just doesn't work for me.

Cold calling sucks because most folks do it wrong. The purpose of a cold call is not to sell, it is to determine the decision maker and set up an appointment to talk to them at a later date. For example, if you are selling advertising and you have done your homework you know certain industries are more likely to advertise with you. If you take the time to scour other media you might find that a potential client already is an advertiser. You might go to the local Chamber website and see if they have a listing of their members and find out the name of the owner. Might even pick up the phone and call and introduce yourself. You might check out their website or Google them to see if what you are offering might meet their needs. Doesn't that sound like a better use of your time then blindly showing up 50 times to make one sale?

The reason that 80% of sales are made on the 5th to the 12th sales call is that folks like to know who they are dealing with. They want to know that you are still around and will keep coming back to find new ways to meet their needs. They want to develop a relationship before they plunk down the cash for your outstanding offering.

My friend, Jim Cathcart, has written several books and has sent me autographed copies of his books, The Acorn Principal, and Relationship Selling. Both are great reference books for developing ongoing customer relations. (I will probably send him a copy of my book now that I think about it!) Jim says in his book that he hates the word cold call and likes to use "introductory call" in its place because that is what it is. It is an opportunity to introduce yourself and what you have to offer and make an appointment to come back. That doesn't mean if the customer is ready to buy on the spot you don't go ahead and close the sale (Jim doesn't like "close" either and prefers "confirm").

So instead of wasting time cold calling try doing some background research. Go to Chamber Business Card Exchanges and do some networking. Don't just exchange cards, get on the phone and follow up with the new folks you meet. The more you get to know them, the more opportunity you have to confirm a sale!

17. IS THERE SUCH A THING AS TOO MUCH?

We try to instill in our students that part of working on your business and not just in it is marketing and of course doing it shamelessly. However there is a point when it can be counterproductive if done to excess. Having run trade and professional associations for many years I know the value of keeping your members happy. A recent example of overdoing it was seen in the recall elections in Wisconsin. The unions who trashed city hall have lost about a third of their members as a result of their actions. They also lost the major elections they were supporting. The Occupy Wall Street gang sure got attention but it was not what they wanted. I only bring those up because they are current and good examples of standing out, but not in an outstanding way.

Businesses can do the same thing by being too "in your face" with their marketing efforts. Geico is a good example of changing their mix. Sure the gecko is cute, but they also offered up the stack of money with the eyeballs, and now the pig with the pinwheel. They rotate their messages to appeal to different audiences. On the other hand we have all seen these almost homemade commercials that feature the owner of a business rambling on about their product or service that nobody has the heart to tell that they are boring. I don't know about you, but I sure wouldn't spend that kind of money for TV ads that can turn customers off.

There are also too cute commercials that make the businesses being touted look unprofessional. I don't have a problem with cute and sometimes funny efforts. I do have a problem with the ones where they just have to get the kids to say a few words so they can see themselves on TV.

Too much also can also apply when selling one on one. Nobody wants to be sold but everybody likes to buy. An overbearing salesperson is a major turn off. Again, no problem with a helpful sales person who assists me in reaching a decision to buy, but the pushy types only push me away.

I'm all for standing out at networking events. But are you doing yourself a favor if you are called on to talk about your business and you stumble over what to say? That is why we drill our students on their elevator speeches. Having a great elevator speech that introduces you to your audience, lets them know what you do, and leaves an opening for them to ask more about your business. It not only gets the message across, it gives you confidence and shows your competency.

The whole point of standing out is to stand out in a way that gets you known but in a positive way. It is ok to do something unique to get attention but not ok if it doesn't reflect positively on what you do. A lawyer in a clown suit is not going to give potential clients much comfort unless the lawyer is performing for a group of kids at a hospital. Context does count!

Stand out, but be outstanding in your efforts.

The choice is between which mistake is easier to correct: underdoing it or overdoing it.
Timothy Geithner

18.SHAMELESS COLLABORATION

Too often, as business owners, we tend to develop the Superman complex. That feeling that you can or must do everything yourself. Fortunately, and I've found this out the hard way, you don't have to do everything yourself.

It is becoming increasingly difficult in recent times, for a small business to go it alone. Scarce resources, time, talent and treasure, are less prevalent than they were just a decade ago. No successful entrepreneur, and that's what most small business owners are, has found success without some reliance or collaboration with others.

These collaborations have allowed entrepreneurs to benefit from resources that are available, but not presently available to them. Small and start up businesses are starting to realize that they are going to need help if they are to survive and in fact, thrive and flourish. One of the places they are seeking and finding help is through small business alliances. Frequently, these small business alliances are nothing more than thinly veiled networking opportunities and done poorly. However, networking, as we will discuss later in the book, is an important and integral part of developing strategic alliances.

What is driving the trend of strategic alliances in almost every industry? They are a way to work together with others toward a common goal while each maintains their individual identity. Economies of scale can play an important role in the why. Strategic collaborations are a way to benefit from a team effort without the additional costs of normal expansion. Businesses get to reap these rewards and all indications are that the rewards can be substantial. Some companies report that as much as 18% of their revenue comes from strategic alliances they have in place.

Monetary gain isn't the only reason to create strategic alliances. Some of the more common reasons are expertise in a market or product, industry convergence, time to market, expanding customer base and increased recognition.

Businesses use strategic alliance to:

➤ Achieve Economies of Scale

➤ Speed to market

➤ Enhanced competitiveness

➤ Enhanced product development

➤ New business opportunities

➤ Expansion of market development

- Diversification

- Create new businesses

- Reduce overall costs

For these and other reasons, collaborations are becoming more and more commonplace for expanding your business' reach without committing undue resources that could be better utilized elsewhere.

Two methods of collaboration are frequently over looked – MasterMind Groups and Peer Groups.

I just listened to a great seminar on CD about how secret societies work. They are all about Mastermind groups that Napoleon Hill talked about in <u>Think and Grow Rich</u>. A key point in the seminar was your willingness to learn. Know-it-alls can't and they miss out on great opportunities to learn. They tend not to be invited back to the next meeting of the Mastermind group. Your openness to learning or teachabilty quotient was a key issue with this instructor.

He noted that there are four levels of competency. The first is unconscious incompetency or the state where you don't know what you don't know. Conscious incompetency is the next level up where you know you don't know but you don't know how to get the knowledge you need. Conscious competency is where you have the basic knowledge to accomplish your goal but have not mastered all the skills. Unconscious competency is when you are on auto-pilot you don't even need to think about the skills necessary to accomplish your goal.

I've heard it said it takes 10,000 times to master a skill. That is why you always see professional golfers practicing shots over and over again so that when the time comes that the shot is needed it will be basically a no-brainer. I've heard the term muscle memory used in this instance but it is more like muscle mastery based on hours of practice.

One of the reasons we started the Entrepreneurial Academy program was to teach small businesses what they don't know they don't know. Many small business owners dive into their business with the technical skills to produce a product or service but are unconsciously incompetent about all the other skills necessary to run a successful business.

Many small business owners do have an awareness of what they don't know and don't know where to go to get the answers they need. With the internet you can Google almost any topic and at least find a launching pad to begin research. There are also outside counselors such as SCORE and SBDC who can provide answers as well as bankers, lawyers, accountants, insurers, and various government agencies.

If you are teachable, you will be able to absorb new direction and change. The seminar leader used the example of learning to tie your shoes. When you first learn how to do it, it may take you a few tries to get it right. Over time you will be practicing and learning about how tight you have to tie the knots and other skills associated with shoe knot tying. You will be developing conscious competency.

After tying your shoes for many years you get to the point where you don't even think about it, you just do it. That is unconscious competence. Or maybe you will just buy loafers and avoid the whole thing entirely! That too is a decision based on what you have learned over time.

The speaker's point was that all of the Mastermind groups have a process for developing their members. You have to master each level in the process before moving on to the next level. You have to be teachable. Everyone who joins the Masons does not become a 33rd Degree Mason.

To sum up the process, you need to be constantly aware of and on the lookout for things that you don't know you don't know. When you find something you don't know that you need to know about, you need to find resources to expand your knowledge. Armed with this new knowledge you need to practice it until you don't have to think about it to do it.

Good design begins with honesty, asks tough questions, comes from collaboration and from trusting your intuition.
Freeman Thomas

19. CAN YOU MAKE IT BETTER?

I recently volunteered for Bowls of Hope, an event to help raise money for the All Faiths Food Bank.. Can't say no to Wendy Namack of Namack Portfolio Investments, LLC. Anybody who knows Wendy knows she is always volunteering her time, talent, and treasure. As a small business owner, it is often hard to say yes to requests for volunteer service. Do it anyway. Consider it part of your public relations package.

If you live and work in a small town your product or service is not the only thing that get's talked about. While you might deliver a great product or service you also have something you can contribute that makes life better for others, your time. No out of pocket costs involved in service.

When my now retired (sorta) partner, Ed Davis and I started the Entrepreneurial Academy, we came to the City of North Port and said to Al Lane, folks are hurting and we need to do something to help them get their businesses up and running and successful. We volunteered our time, talent, and treasure to make it happen. We have some success stories from our graduates that we love to brag on. Want to know what is also great, "Our Kids", are also out volunteering their time assisting area non-profit organizations like the Chamber and The City and Vision North Port and there were a couple volunteering along with me at Bowls of Hope.

Back when Ed was working with the Charlotte Community Foundation he asked me to speak at a luncheon on Volunteers. I talked to the overflow crowd about the "3R's of Volunteer Management". They were Recruitment, Retention, and Reward. Some of the association executives in the room had a problem with the last R. There was a feeling that being a part of their valuable organization was reward in and of itself. Granted, for some folks that does work, they get an ego stroke being affiliated with an organization that does good. My point was, that volunteers do what they do for their own return on investment. If you don't know what that return to them is, good luck with the Recruitment and Retention parts.

People volunteer for their own reasons in other words, their return on the investment of their time. Many folks for example will invest their time, talent, and treasure for cancer research because a family member or friend had a situation with it. For some folks it is just something to do in retirement. For small business owners, unless it is a personal commitment, there needs to be a return on investment. Often it doesn't need to be much, a personal relationship, networking opportunities, maybe even a picture in your local paper! Doesn't matter, it is their reward and if you are recruiting volunteers you need to find what floats their boat.

There are hundreds of local organizations that would not exist if it were not for their volunteers. I grew up in a family that was constantly volunteering their time to organizations in need of help. My Mom spent her last day on earth at Tidewell Hospice where she was a volunteer. I've served on the Board of Directors of the Boys and Girls Clubs of Greater Washington, DC, and about 15 other voluntary boards, most of which even cost me money to participate on because I believed in what they were doing. I've raised money for non-profits and started three 501c3 organizations myself.

For many of my friends, this is the first time they have ever heard any of this about me. I don't make a big deal any more about anything I personally do. I just don't care about the past. Yes, I do shamelessly market everything I have my name attached to because if I didn't, my Dad's Ghost would haunt me. Also because I have a great (and getting better) time doing it. I've been giving away my time gratis for years to help out friends. My return on investment is letting them know if they need a friend they have one in me. Ask for my help, if I can do it you got it. If I can't I'll tell you why. I'm easy, I'll do what I can to help a friend.

So find a cause you care about and invest yourself in it. It's all good. Volunteer, you can make a difference. You might even get a bowl of soup or two for your efforts. I did!

THURGOOD MARSHALL

NONE OF US HAS GOTTEN WHERE WE ARE SOLELY BY PULLING OURSELVES UP FROM OUR OWN BOOTSTRAPS. WE GOT HERE BECAUSE SOMEBODY BENT DOWN AND HELPED US.

21. BEING REMEMBERED

There are two sides to being remembered. Your side and your clients' side. Let's look at your side first. You have a business or you work for one. Some companies and people have instant name recognition. That's what you're striving for. Do you remember Park Taehwan? Most people don't. But they do remember Michael Phelps. Michael Phelps won the 200 meter freestyle race at the 2008 Olympics (among other events). Park Taehwan came a close second.

With the possible exception of Avis (we're #2, we try harder), people like number one. They want the best. Unfortunately, there can only be one best. With that being said, people still like number one. It could be the fastest, hottest, the coldest, tallest, the most, the strangest, the coolest.

We don't need to limit ourselves to strictly the biggest or the best. If you are a retailer, can you compete with the buying and negotiating ability of Wal-Mart? Probably not, but you can still distinguish yourself and your business. Can you provide the fastest service , the quickest response times, the hottest food, the newest products?

Can you be the most caring business? Simple things can get you to stand out. But when you do stand out in such a way, you need to capitalize on it and promote the heck out of it.

Let everyone know. WE"RE #1, in whatever it is you are number one at.

I have friends that protested the fact Wal-Mart was moving into the area. I was a little baffled. Contrary to popular belief, they don't put otherwise healthy small businesses out of business.

They have to get creative and compete on something other than price. Let's face it, Wal-Mart may not always have the lowest price on something, but overall, you are not going to compete on price, and you shouldn't anyway. When you compete on price, you become just another commodity.

In fact, having the largest retailer move to an area, helps small businesses de-commoditize. The small businesses re-learn what really sets them apart. Wal-Mart may have low prices, but you have the friendliest staff, the easiest contacts, fastest turnaround. Whether you have large competition moving next door or not, identify where you are number one. And use it to your advantage.

The other side of being remembered is from your customers perspective. The first word in the AIDA principle is Attention. What are you doing to attract attention to your business? Our concept of "Shameless Marketing" is whatever it takes to attract attention to you in a positive manner. Note the word "positive" because you can attract a world of hurt on the negative side.

Last year I joked about getting attention by putting on a pizza outfit and dancing on US 41 to attract attention to Old Monty's Pizza Well somebody must be reading my column because I saw not one, but two dancing pizza slices on my way home this evening. We are taking marketing to the streets in a creative effort to thwart restictive sign laws. We are that creative. In Englewood, The Country Hound Restaurant has a waving hound dog. There are numerous Liberty Tax wavers out this tax season as well as Android phone sign wavers and "we buy gold" wavers. As we gear up for the next election we are seeing more and more political sign wavers out on local street corners. The Girl Scouts were out and about in their uniforms at local shopping centers promoting cookie sales. Not a weekend goes by that there isn't at least one high school group out promoting a car wash and waving signs along the highway.

Whatever works to bring positive attention to your business is OK with me. Do it and do it shamelessly. Let the world know you exist and attract attention to your business and location.

Another thing I'm seeing more of are car wraps and rear window signs along with a plethora of political bumper stickers. This is fine too with the exception of the promotional stuff on a vehicle that looks like it is on life support. If your rolling billboard looks like a demolition derby survivor you are saying something about your business you really don't want folks to know.

The image you are projecting for your business can speak louder than you do. If you are a service provider and you show up at my house with a company vehicle and park it outside my place you are telling my neighbors something about me in my choice of your service. If that vehicle, boldly touting your business name, looks like a loser in a local mud run or something Fred Flintstone would be embarrassed to drive, you are attracting attention both to you as a business and me as a customer; none of it good.

More and more businesses are providing their employees with logo shirts. Nothing wrong with that unless of course the shirt is battered or looks like you got into a fight with a pig and the pig won.

How about your printed materials, brochures, business cards, flyers, print ads, do they all tie together and look sharp? These are your silent salesmen that can work for you or against you if they all don't positively continue your message. Ever get a business card from someone that had writing all over the back of it? I have, and it doesn't project a positive image in my mind.

How about your personal appearance and your team's look, are they sharp and well groomed or do they look like bouncers at a strip club? I went into a restaurant one time where the waitress had so many face piercings I lost my appetite.

All these things and more speak loudly to people's perception of you and your business. Years ago, when I was selling advertising for Harbor Style Magazine, I started out making sales calls in a suit and tie. I quickly learned that in Southwest Florida when you show up dressed like that folks assume you are a banker or a salesman. I went out and bought a whole new wardrobe of Hawaiian shirts and nice slacks and it changed folks' perception of me and added a flair of Florida that we were selling at the magazine.

Go promote your business shamelessly, but also with pride. Have fun but show some class in the process. Get prospects attention in a positive way. It all goes to the bottom line and there is nothing shameful in that!

IF YOU WOULD NOT BE FORGOTTEN AS SOON AS YOU ARE DEAD, EITHER WRITE THINGS WORTH READING OR DO THINGS WORTH WRITING.

BENJAMIN FRANKLIN

BONUS CHAPTER – LIVE!

Just listened to a TED video of Steve Jobs giving a commencement address at Stanford called "How to Live Before You Die" http://www.ted.com/talks/steve_jobs_how_to_live_before_y ou_die.html. One of the great lines in his talk concerned something he read that said "If you live each day as if it were your last…eventually you will be right".

Jobs talked about dropping out of college, starting Apple in his garage, getting fired, and starting over with two new companies Next and Pixar. What struck me was how he used that saying of living each day as if it were your last to get up each morning and ask himself if he was happy about what he was going to do that day. If the answer was no he knew it was time for a change in his life.

That is a great philosophy. If you can't be happy about what you are doing that day, ask yourself why the heck you are doing it or what needs to change to make it enjoyable.

In another TED video Robert Chapman, Chairman and CEO of Barry-Wehmiller Companies points out that 88% of people who get up each morning and go to work are not happy about the prospect. He instituted what he calls a

"People Centric" philosophy in his company that recognizes employees in many ways for what they do. His point was made by one of his employees who was invited to address a management conference on a very successful project he had just completed. Chapman asked him how this project had changed his life and he answered that he was talking to his wife more.

What Chapman realized was that corporate America for years hired folks to just work with their hands. By not recognizing the10 good things that employees did and raising holy hell when they did something wrong he was placing stress on the employees. He now has employees vote by division for who among their peers did a great job this year and he awards them a new car. His point was that by raising recognition he was able to also get not just the hands of employees but their hearts and minds. One of the measures he uses to track his success now among his thousands of employees is the divorce rate. He noted that people who are not happy in their work bring it home with them and it affects their home lives. It reminds me of the poem that goes,

It's not my job to run the train
Or even clang the bell.
But watch the danged thing jump the track
And see who catches hell.

I realize the economy is not great and many folks are doing work because they have to, not because they want to and it is something they love to do. I've come to a point in my life where I agree with Jobs' philosophy, if I'm not happy about what is on my plate for the day, I'm getting a new plate because some day as Jobs did I'll be right also. Don't just exist, live!

22. 50 SHAMELESS STRATEGIES

1. **Follow Up**. We all know we should, but most don't. Following up will certainly set you apart from the competition.

2. **Have Business Cards**. Have them with you all the time. In your pocket, in your purse, in your portfolio, in your car. You never know when you'll bump into that next marketing moment. If you are prepared, you'll stand out.

3. **Write articles**. The perception is that only experts write articles. Become the expert. Write a useful article for your local paper, a trade magazine, or anywhere your target audience is reading. Experts stand out.

4. **Write books**. If you think writing articles builds your credibility (and it does) try writing a book. You have tons more credibility. Don't think you have it in you? Repurpose the articles you wrote in Strategy 3.

5. **Give talks**. There are a lot of organizations in your community that need people to speak at their functions. I'm not talking about seminars or arenas. Lunch meetings, chamber meetings, Rotary meetings, etc. They not only add to your credibility, but get you

in front of potential referral sources and can really boost your confidence. Confident people stand out.

6. **Write columns**. This is just like writing articles, except you are doing it a regular basis. More exposure, more credibility, more perceived expertise.

7. **Networking**. You'll notice that we didn't call it socializing with your peeps at a sponsored event. Networking is so much more. We have a chapter devoted to it in this book. There are some good books written about and how to do it right. In fact, we are in the processing of writing one on Shameless Networking.

8. **Write (relevant) blogs**. These are usually quick, easy and build credibility.

9. **Join LinkedIn**. Don't just join. Join relevant groups and contribute. Many join, few contribute.

10. **Volunteer**. People like people that give back. You get to become known in your community.

11. **Join a peer group**. Can't find one. Start one. According to research by Dun & Bradstreet professional peer members were **two and one-half times more productive** than non-members. That sounds pretty outstanding to me.

12. **Hire a coach**. Athletes, actors, CEOs, managers, business owners all hire coaches to get them to the next level. Want to be at your peak. A coach can help.

13. **Continue learning**. Whether it's professional development or personal development, never stop learning and evolving. It will keep you ahead of the pack.

14. **Cold Call.** There are a lot fewer people and businesses doing this today. We've heard all the reasons (excuses) for this, but most come down to call reluctance. People don't like rejection. Get over it. It's part of business. Go knock on some doors.

15. **Develop Systems.** Life is easier and clients are happier when there is consistency. Have you ever gone back to a restaurant that served you a great meal only to find that this meal was less than ideal? Consistency. Systems create consistency. Consistency helps you stand out in a positive manner.

16. **Raise your prices.** If you are providing the service and providing the value an additional 5% to bottom line is a good thing.

17. **Collaborate.** There are no rules that say you have to do it all on your own. Are there complementary businesses that you can work with to benefit both of you?

18. **Prioritize Your Clients/Prospects.** Remember the 80/20 rule. 80% of your business comes from 20% of your clients.

19. **Do Surveys.** What do people want. Ask them.

20. **Vehicle Wraps.** Nothing says "Look at me" quite like a traveling billboard.

21. **Have a Facebook Business Page.** With more than 800,000,000 active participants, it just makes sense to be in the mix.

22. **Put videos on YouTube.** Short informational videos can help people and help get you noticed.

23. **Wear Name Tags.** Quietly lets people know who you are and what you do.

24. **Use media releases.** A little self promotion goes a long way.

25. **Do radio and TV interviews.** There are a lot of local radio and TV stations that need good stories and good content. Be that story, provide that content.

26. **Use integrity.** Doing the right thing even when no one is looking.

27. **Send thank you notes.** When was the last time you got a hand written thank you from someone? Never? It will truly set you apart.

28. **Be a Sponsor.** Tons of good organizations need financial support. Sponsoring one of their events is a great way to help them and get you recognized as a community leader.

29. **Give samples.** Let's people test drive your product or service.

30. **Have a great elevator speech.** Quickly let people know who you are, what you do and how you can help them.

31. **Be enthusiastic.** Nothing creates credibility quite like you being enthusiastic about what you do.

32. **Use Twitter.** Make it part of your social media marketing campaign.

33. **Send an e-newsletter.** Keep in touch with your clients regularly and give them the information that makes their lives better or easier.

34. **Use coupons.** Easy to make. Easy to distribute. Easy to redeem.

35. **Smile.** A smile breaks the ice and shows you are happy to be there.

36. **Hand out tchotchkes.** Inexpensive and can be handed out just about anywhere and anytime.

37. **Wear logoed attire.** Shirts, hats, jackets – put your name and logo on them.

38. **Utilize costumed characters.** Ever seen a slice of pizza waving at you on the side of the road?

39. **Create brochures.** Space for the information that didn't fit on your business card.

40. **Rent a billboard.** Picture your message 12 feet high.

41. **Telemarket.** Old fashioned, but efficient and effective.

42. **Media Advertising.** Advertise where your target market is.

43. **Define your target market.** What does your ideal client look like?

44. **Ask for the business.** Eventually, you have to ask them to do business with you.

45. **Use Pinterest.** One of the newer social media platforms is gaining in popularity.

46. **Join industry associations.** A great way to expand your reach and your message.

47. **Use a marketing calendar.** Marketing effectiveness varies. This will help you keep your message consistent.

48. **Track your marketing.** What's working, what's not. If you don't track it, you'll never know.

49. **Send and post photos.** A picture is worth a thousand words.

50. **Try something out of the ordinary.** Get out of your comfort zone.

51. **Give them more than they expect.** Promise and then exceed expectations

ABOUT THE AUTHORS

Mickey Gorman has over 40 years experience working with small businesses and nonprofit organizations. He has owned and operated his own consulting and management firm, managed several professional associations and provided consulting services to other organizations. Mickey became one of the youngest Certified Association Executives at the age of 29 and maintained the designation for 30 years.

A sales and marketing pro, Mickey brings more than 40 years of real world experience to the audience. Author of many white papers and sales and marketing programs, including "Savvy Selling". Mickey is a partner and founding member of Small Business Development Services, LLC, which designs, develops and delivers training programs. Mickey can be contacted at mickeygorman@live.com or 941-661-4802.

Brendon Sommers – Brendon has been selling and training salespeople for more than 30 years. He is a highly regarded speaker and trainer. Brendon brings a fresh clear perspective to creatively growing businesses through networking, strategic alliances and a comprehensive , customized sales training program. Brendon is a partner and founding member of Your Team, LLC, which designs and delivers customized sales training programs and small business consulting. Brendon Sommers can be contacted at 941-544-3981 or brendon.sommers@yourteamfla.com

www.ingramcontent.com/pod-product-compliance
Lightning Source LLC
Chambersburg PA
CBHW051336170526
45166CB00002B/835